UNDERSTANDING BIOMASS ENERGY

IMPORTANCE OF BIOFUELS

BIOMASS ENERGY FOR KIDS
CHILDREN'S ECOLOGY BOOKS

BABY PROFESSOR

EDUCATION KIDS

Speedy Publishing LLC

40 E. Main St. #1156

Newark, DE 19711

www.speedypublishing.com

Copyright 2017

In this book, we're going to talk all about biomass energy. So, let's get right to it!

WHAT IS RENEWABLE ENERGY?

Petroleum and coal are non-renewable forms of energy. The reason is that once they are taken from the Earth it will take millions of years for them to form again. These types of non-renewable forms are called "fossil fuels" and they produce carbon compounds that pollute the air and water.

OIL REFINERY PLANT

BIOMASS HEATING POWER PLANT

owever, there are forms of energy such as hydroelectric power and solar power that just require energy from water sources and the sun. These types of energy sources are called renewable. Biomass energy is a renewable source of energy as well.

In order for an energy source to be considered renewable it has to have these two major characteristics:

- Its source shouldn't run out or if it does run out it should be able to be replaced
- Its source should be "carbon neutral," which simply means that it doesn't create carbon compounds when it is used

RENEWABLE ENERGY

EMISSIONS FROM COAL POWER PLANT

In addition, most renewable forms of energy either don't pollute the environment or they have minimal environmental impact compared to fossil fuels.

WHAT IS BIOMASS ENERGY?

If you've ever burned wood in a fireplace or outdoors on a campground, then you've used biomass energy to generate heat. Biomass is basically any substance that is created by either plants or animals and that can be transformed into energy and used for fuel.

When you see the word "biomass," you can connect it to the word "biology." The energy that biomass holds in storage is energy that came from the sun originally.

The sun's light and warmth gives plants energy, which they convert to sugars using a process called photosynthesis. In essence, plants are their own "food factories."

This energy is held in the plant material even after the plant dies. Animals get energy from the sun indirectly because they eat the plants that have stored up the sun's energy. There's even energy in the wastes that animals eliminate, such as manure.

MANURE

BIOMASS IS A RENEWABLE FORM OF ENERGY

Energy from biomass is considered to be renewable, because as long as there's a sun, the Earth, water and nutrients, we can grow additional plants or trees. However, renewable doesn't mean infinite since there is a limit to land and water resources.

WHAT TYPES OF MATERIALS CAN BE CONVERTED INTO BIOMASS ENERGY?

Lots of different types of materials can be transformed into biomass energy. A large proportion of biomass energy in the United States comes from wood and wood products. Corn and sugar cane are other popular sources for conversion to biomass energy in the form of ethanol.

SUGAR CANE

Manure from animals and even garbage we throw out, such as food scraps and lawn clippings, can be used as sources of biomass energy.

THE HISTORY OF BIOMASS ENERGY

Biomass energy isn't new. Ever since man figured out how to use fire to generate heat, wood has been burned to keep warm. Even today, around the world, many people still use wood as their main source of heating during the cold winter months. In the United States in the 1800s, ethanol was used to fuel lamps before electric lights were invented and made popular.

FUEL LAMPS

Some of the first automobiles, Model-T Fords, were powered on ethanol instead of gasoline until the year 1908. Today, biofuels are seen as a better alternative to using non-renewable fossil fuels like gasoline.

HOW DO WE CONVERT BIOMASS TO BIOMASS ENERGY?

There are many different ways to convert biomass to biomass energy.

BURNING

If you burn wood, you release energy from it. The heat from burning wood or other forms of biomass is used to increase the temperature inside homes or buildings during cold months.

The heat generated from burning can also be used to make steam, which can be used to create electrical power for other types of applications, such as powering electrical motors.

CONVERSION OF METHANE GAS

If you've ever been near a landfill, then you know how bad methane gas smells. When garbage or other forms of biomass decay they give off methane gas. The good news is that this smelly gas is very useful. It can be converted into natural gas, which is used for heating, for generating electricity, and for cooking. It can also be used as a fuel for vehicles and many other applications in manufacturing.

CREATION OF BIOFUELS

A few types of crops, such as corn or sugar cane, can be transformed into ethanol, which is a type of biofuel. Ethanol is

a substitute for gasoline and works to power many different types of cars. The process of fermentation that is used to create ethanol is described as gasification.

Biodiesel is another form of biofuel. It's created from the fat of animals as well as vegetable oil and can be used to generate heat or to run vehicles, such as cars, trucks, and buses.

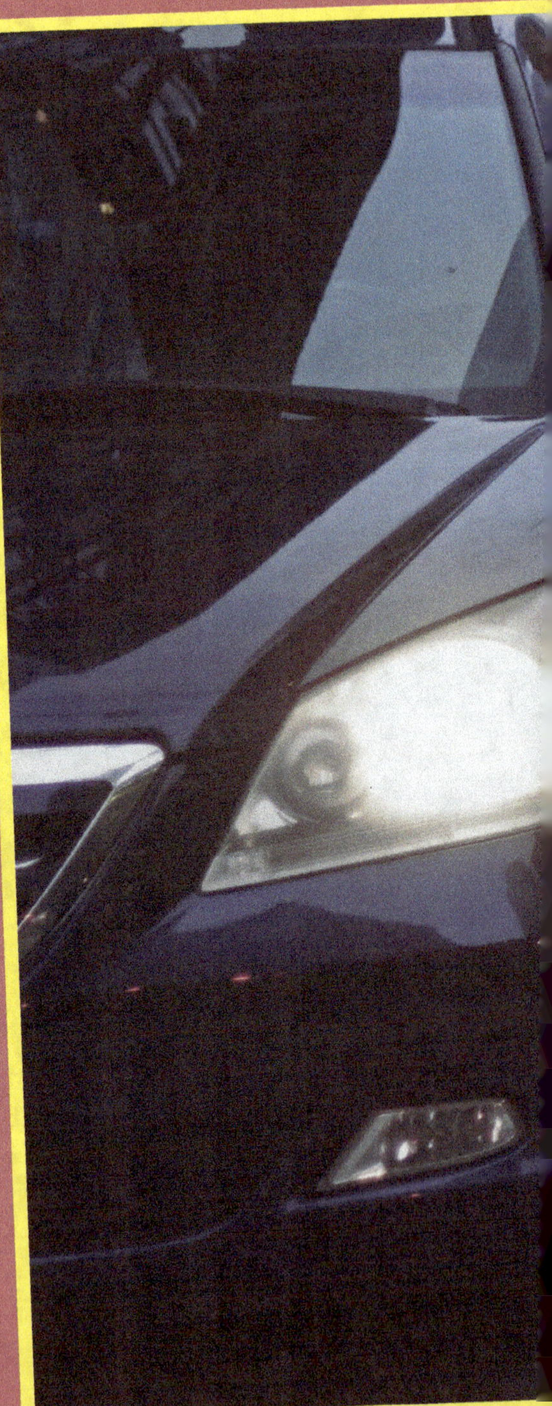

CARS

ARE THERE ANY DISADVANTAGES TO BIOMASS ENERGY?

There are some disadvantages to using biomass to create energy.

- Burning frequently creates air pollution, which releases carbon dioxide and other potentially harmful gases into the air

AIR POLLUTION

- Harmful chemicals and potentially harmful gases are sometimes released into the air from burning biomass waste and trash

- In order to grow crops that can be converted into biofuels, trees have to be cut down and the land has to be cleared of native vegetation, which sometimes destroys animal and plant habitats

The land that's designated for biomass crops potentially takes land away that may be needed for food crops.

- Growing biomass crops requires chemical fertilizers, which if not properly handled can cause pollution of runoff waters.

Despite these disadvantages, many people believe that biomass energy and biofuels are worth pursuing as energy sources instead of non-renewable sources such as coal and oil. Scientists are continuously working to make these forms of biomass energy less polluting.

HOW IS BIOMASS ENERGY TRANSFORMED INTO USABLE ELECTRICITY?

The process of converting biomass energy through burning uses several steps.

STEP 1

The sun's energy is stored in plants. When the plants die or are cut down the plant material is brought to a storage bunker. The plant matter can be chips of wood, clippings, or straw.

WOOD CHIPS

STEP 2

The plant material is burned to increase the water temperature in a boiler. When the water is boiled, it emits heat energy in the form of steam.

STEP 3

The steam power is channeled through pipes to turbines.

STEP 4

The blades of the turbines are turned by the steam. The turbines power electrical generators, which are constructed from coils as well as magnets.

WIND TURBINES

The magnetic fields become charged, which produces electricity.

STEP 6

The electricity travels through cables to get to your home or your school where it can be used to power the lights, the heat, or appliances.

HOW MUCH BIOMASS ENERGY IS USED WORLDWIDE?

Biomass is used more frequently than any other type of energy source after oil, natural gas, and coal. It accounts for more than 10% of the world's energy sources.

PILE OF BAGS WITH BIOMASS FORMED IN PELLETS

BIOGAS PLANT

INTERESTING FACTS ABOUT BIOMASS ENERGY

- Farmers use special tanks known as digesters to produce biogas from livestock manure. Electricity can be generated using biogas.

- Gasoline in the United States is a blend of fuels including ethanol.

- Waste-to-Energy is the name of the process where garbage that people throw out is burned and converted to energy. One advantage of waste-to-energy is that it decreases the quantity of trash that ends up in permanent landfills.
- Biodiesel is currently the most popular fuel alternative to gasoline in the United States.
- Sugar from crops is the essential component needed to make ethanol fuel. Any crop that contains a high proportion of sugar can be used to make it. Barley and rice are two crops that have been used, but even clippings from certain grasses can be used.

BARLEY

EUCALYPTUS TREES

- Biomass is expected to increase as an energy source in the coming decades.
- In the future, human waste might be used as a source of biomass energy. Scientists at Penn State University have created a machine that can produce 51 kilowatts of energy from the waste produced by 100,000 people.
- Tree species that grow very fast, such as eucalyptus trees and poplar trees, are currently being considered as crops to be grown specifically for biomass.
- It's possible that in the future biofuels will completely eliminate the need for fossil fuels such as gasoline.

SUMMARY

Biomass energy is a form of renewable energy along with solar, wind and water. Plants and animals use energy from the sun and that energy can be converted to energy that people can use to heat their homes and power their vehicles and machines. Even though the process to convert biomass into biomass energy and fuels does create some pollution, many people think it should continue to be developed as an alternative to highly polluting fossil fuels.

Awesome! Now that you've read about biomass energy you may want to read about other types of renewable energy in the Baby Professor book *An Introduction to Renewable Energy Sources.*

MASS ENERGY

Visit
BABY PROFESSOR
EDUCATION KIDS
www.BabyProfessorBooks.com
to download Free Baby Professor eBooks
and view our catalog of new and exciting
Children's Books